SEATTLE'S USED BOOKSTORES: 1999 AND 2019

A LOVE NOTE TO BOOK
CULTURE AND THE PRE-DIGITAL AGE

Photos and Text by

MARY BROWN

Copyright © 2023 Mary Brown.

All rights reserved. No part of this book may be reproduced, stored, or transmitted by any means—whether auditory, graphic, mechanical, or electronic—without written permission of both publisher and author, except in the case of brief excerpts used in critical articles and reviews. Unauthorized reproduction of any part of this work is illegal and is punishable by law.

All rights to the text, images, photographs, and other content are owned by the author. Except as expressly stated in this Agreement, you may not copy, reproduce, change, distribute, or transmit any of the contents.

ISBN: 979-8-88640-652-8 (sc)
ISBN: 979-8-88640-662-7 (hc)
ISBN: 979-8-88640-471-5 (e)

Because of the dynamic nature of the Internet, any web addresses or links contained in this book may have changed since publication and may no longer be valid. The views expressed in this work are solely those of the author and do not necessarily reflect the views of the publisher, and the publisher hereby disclaims any responsibility for them.

One Galleria Blvd., Suite 1900, Metairie, LA 70001
1-888-421-2397

CONTENTS

Dedication v
Acknowledgments vii
Introduction ix

Chapter 1   Twice Sold Tales, Capitol Hill 1
Chapter 2   Magus Books, University District 22
Chapter 3   BLMF Books and Lamplight Books,
            Pike Place Market 43
Chapter 4   The Globe and Arundel Books, Pioneer Square ...55
Chapter 5   Ophelia's Books, Fremont 72
Chapter 6   Couth Buzzard Books, Greenwood 82

Conclusion 91
Appendix 97
Endnotes 101

DEDICATION

For Mom (the painter), Dad (the builder), and Jessie (the reader).

For Tommy, whose readings of *Taffy Sinclair* I will never forget.

For Gus and Penny.

And in memoriam, John Stamets (1949–2014), Seattle's photographer.

Elizabeth Reutlinger, my mother, in an unidentified downtown Seattle bookstore, 1999.

ACKNOWLEDGMENTS

I am very grateful to all the bookstore owners who permitted me to photograph their stores, answered questions, and wished the project well. I would also like to acknowledge the people in the photographs, readers and booksellers, who are not named, as they are the essential part of the ecology of bookstores and create some of the most interesting photographs.

Charles Fischer's 2013 article, "Seattle's Disappearing Bookstores," from *Seattle Magazine*, is a gem of insight into his experience working in a used bookstore and is quoted at length herein.

Special thanks to Roxi Kringle for her excellent feedback on the photos and essays as well as unfailing warmth and good cheer as a friend and neighbor. Elizabeth Reutlinger, my mother, helped fine-tune the final draft by freeing me of my attachment to commas, semi-colons, and unnecessary phrases.

Further thanks are due to Ellen and Tom Flynn of the Art Establishment in Bethlehem, Pennsylvania, for operating a multipurpose art studio with a first-rate darkroom, the only public darkroom within a ninety-mile radius. Dan's Camera City in Allentown also deserves credit for not giving up on the print and continuing to sell photo paper, even if it is kept in a backroom closet.

To contain the project within workable boundaries, several unique bookplaces in Seattle have been omitted: Lion Heart Bookstore and Left Bank Books in Pike Place Market (a mix of new and used books), Mercer Street Books in Queen Anne, Pegasus Book Exchange in West Seattle, Twice Sold Tales in Ballard, Horizon Books on First Hill, the three locations of Third Place Books (new and used) in Ravenna, Seward Park, and Lake Forest Park, Estelita's Library and Bookstore between the Central District and Leschi Park, and B. Brown and Associates between Fremont and Northlake. Sea Ocean Books, once a neighbor to B. Brown selling rare naval and marine-themed titles, shuttered at the end of 2019. All of these places have stories and collections as interesting and valuable as those featured in this project, and I hope my readers will discover them.

INTRODUCTION

There is no death, only a change of worlds.
—Chief Seattle

*Don't it always seem to go, that you don't
know what you've got 'til it's gone.*
—Joni Mitchell

If you are taking in these words, you already understand something about why this project came into being and recognize the pleasure and edification obtained through reading. Every book is a conduit to other worlds of thought and experience that, once assimilated, become permanent mental keepsakes. While the magic may reside in the books, the libraries, bookstores, and personal collections that house them possess their own transformative power. Book-filled spaces offer both a refuge from exterior chaos and the thrill of possibility within their rows and nooks. Fiction, mystery, world art, religion, sexuality, biography, gardening, parenting, humor, horror, and countless more topics are ensconced in portable, often beautifully designed and illustrated bundles possessing a pleasing tactile permanence.

Seattle's Used Bookstores celebrates one element of book culture: the used bookstore. My aim is to show, in photographs and brief essays, what makes used bookstores unique and interesting, to reflect on their contribution to urban street life and the larger community, and to recognize what is lost when they disappear. Used bookstores provide a brush with the numinous rarely found within other venues, as they possess a particular alchemy of time and place: the lives of their books and the setting in which to explore them. Used bookstores also remind us that there is much to appreciate about the experience of slowing down, making the effort to visit places outside of home and work, stumbling upon the unexpected, and finding a book—or five, ten, or twenty—by interacting with another person.

SEATTLE

Seattle, Washington, is situated in one of the country's most extraordinary landscapes. Rugged and silvery, the Pacific Northwest's mountains and sea have long been the area's backbone and lifeblood. The city grew up on a series of steep hills and rocky shorelines between salt and fresh water, with the Salish Sea to the west and twenty-two-mile-long Lake Washington to the east. As the Emerald City of the Evergreen State—so named for its many varieties of conifers—Seattle is replete with trees that appear to blanket all but its downtown business district. Further to the east stretch the snowy peaks of the Cascade Range, and looking west across Elliot Bay, the sun sets over the Olympic Mountains. Lake Union, with its human-made canal system connecting the Salish Sea to Lake Washington, opens up the land just north of the downtown business center, creating an expansive oasis tucked right into the urban environment.

This stunning setting, coupled with Seattle's series of hills, means that water and mountains are rarely out of sight. Traces of wildness can still be felt in even the most urbanized zones: a blast of salt air from an early spring squall on downtown's bustling First Avenue, the smell of the trees along numerous urban greenbelts, and tangles of blackberry bushes making their way into otherwise well-kept lawns and urban landscapes. Washington State Ferries carry thousands of people a day across the Salish Sea, accompanied by seagulls, often porpoises, and occasionally southern resident orcas. Travelers are seen off and greeted by cormorant colonies gathered on the waterfront dock pilings. Seattle's oceanic climate creates a long, prolific growing season, spectacular sunbursts throughout the year, and clear, cool summer air. It also brings in the area's rain and infamous gray cloud cover that lasts from early fall to late spring, from which Seattleites find comfort in coffee, movies, chocolate, and—of course—books.[1]

PROJECT ORIGINS: SEATTLE, 1999

At the turn of the last millennium, Seattle was in a comfortably mellow lull following a surge of cultural and commercial activity. Grunge music, born in the northwest in the eighties as an underground, alternative sound, had become wildly popular and commercially successful by the middle of the nineties. A building boom from 1990 to 1997 brought significant new construction to the downtown district, including five new skyscrapers, the Seattle Art Museum, and a bus tunnel. Starbucks Coffee, hatched in Seattle's Pike Place Market in 1971, was already a national chain and poised on the brink of global domination, yet dozens of smaller, independent coffee shops were still thriving. The University of Washington had opened new campuses in nearby Bothell and Tacoma and continued to lead the world in fields such as medicine, computer science, and engineering. Bookstores, used and new, seemed to be everywhere.[2] University Way, the main thoroughfare in in the university district, had five stores selling only used books.

The internet and its World Wide Web had entered life, work, and study ("information superhighway" was already a cliché, email was a primary medium of communication), but it was still mostly populated by individual pages that were developed slowly and required coding knowledge to create. Some problems were already surfacing (e.g., web addiction, pornography, the caustic rants of people feeling emboldened by their anonymity and the safe distance of the screen). Websites were not used as sources in academic papers due to the difficulty of verifying the information most of them contained. Nevertheless, "the web" was generally seen as a welcome tool for communication and exchange of information.

In 1999, I was a twenty-year-old art history major attending the University of Washington, Seattle, where I had the good fortune to explore and develop a longtime interest in photography. I was particularly attracted to the lines, patterns, and details of architecture. During the previous summer of 1998, I completed an introductory course in architectural photography taught by John Stamets (1949–2014). After thoroughly enjoying this introductory course, I made my way into his seminar, "Special Projects in Architectural Photography," which required one in-depth photo essay exploring built environments, rendered in a unifying aesthetic.

I thought of used bookstores right away. Libraries are magnificent (the University of Washington contains one of the world's largest library systems, including the stunning 1922 Collegiate Gothic Suzzallo Library Reading Room), but they also house the miasma of long hours of study and oppressive quantities of required reading, limit public access, and tend to discourage mingling between visitors in order to maintain a studious atmosphere. The big-box chains Borders and Barnes and Noble, while also enjoyable, were so full of peripheral merchandise that some were barely recognizable as bookstores. Independent bookstores selling new books, such as Seattle's famous Elliot Bay Books, also came to mind, as they are lovely, elegant places and host a multitude of community events, but many still retain a degree of formality that can affect a visitor's experience.

The used bookstore, on the other hand, provides a sense of comfort and accessibility that invites one to look, read, and stay for a while, without the fear of being barked at to *stop browsing and buy*, while the randomness of books themselves can lead to adventure and discovery far from the bestseller lists. Out-of-print titles, early editions with dated cover art, the offbeat—it is all there, sometimes only costing a quarter or two. The books themselves are enhanced, not diminished, by their path through others' lives. There is also a brush with the bittersweet within the spaces, as they can evoke loss, awareness of time passed, and the fleeting nature of human happiness. Books are often given up due to difficult life events and transitions, such as death, divorce, moving, or financial hardship. In "Seattle's Disappearing Bookstores," Charles Fischer notes,

> Used books bear the mark of time on their dust jackets, spines, and pages: the underlined notes of a hopeful reader that drop off after the first chapter, the dedications, inscriptions, and signatures of past owners, many of whom presumably are now dead. …
>
> Unlike new books, pre-owned books are often a story wrapped in another story. Once while culling through a library full of books, Magus clerk Maureen Duryee found a cache of love letters from a University of Washington professor to his recently deceased wife. 'When I gave the box of letters to him, he held them like a baby,' she says. A few weeks later, the professor came into the store. Duryee remembers him saying, 'When I got them back, I closed all the curtains to my living room, read the letters and spent three days with my wife.'[3]

John Koenig's online *Dictionary of Obscure Sorrows*, a collection of invented words meant to capture complex, melancholic emotions, includes the entry *vellichor*.

> **vellichor** (noun): the strange wistfulness of used bookstores, which are somehow infused with the passage of time—filled with thousands of old books you'll never have time to read, each of which is itself locked in its own era, bound and dated and papered over like an old room the author abandoned years ago, a hidden annex littered with thoughts left just as they were on the day they were captured.[4]

Further, the sight of a 1950s-era hardback might trigger an unexpected rush of grief for a deceased parent or grandparent whose home was filled with similar books. *Vellichor* also acknowledges the stab of sadness one feels in the presence of so many books, knowing that there is never enough time in one life to read them all. The stacks and titles are also humbling reminders of the depth of history and range of human experience, all there is yet to learn, and how much mystery remains in the world.

The project was approved, although I was advised to keep an eye on the structure of the spaces and cautioned against including too many treacly cat photos. It ultimately became more of a photojournalistic look at people within these spaces and less of an architectural essay. Nevertheless, the project was judged to be a success, and I hoped to one day create a book with some of the photographs. The 1999 photographs are all darkroom printed from hand-developed film, rendered in a low-contrast, subdued light befitting interiors and the quiet act of reading. As products of film and the darkroom, they are also vestiges of the pre-digital age. Before digital photography, exposed film rolls were developed by hand in canisters with carefully calibrated water temperatures and chemical mixtures, hung to dry in dustproof lockers, then trimmed, packaged into clear, plastic negative holders, and turned into contact sheets in the darkroom. Compared to digital photography, it was a slow, cumbersome process.

Film photography, however, still has its own special appeal. Many photographers take more pride in one quality print than hundreds of images captured on a digital camera or smartphone. The palpable click of a camera's shutter at a chosen moment, the excitement of pulling developed film off a plastic reel, and watching an image slowly emerge on paper in the surreal light of a darkroom cannot be experienced in digital work. As frustrating as the darkroom process can be, the manual craft of it—dodging and burning light, selecting contrast filters, and the slight element of chance that influences the outcome—adds to its artistry and magic. The 1999 photographs included here were taken with a boxy, metal Pentax 35mm film camera made sometime in the 1980s, whose light meter was a floating needle nudged into equilibrium with adjustments to the aperture and shutter. Having reluctantly accepted digital photography around 2005, I took the 2019 photos with a Canon digital camera and edited them with Adobe's Lightroom software.

SEATTLE, 2019: TECH BOOM OR TECH BOMB?

From 1999 to 2019, both Seattle and the world have changed more rapidly than most of us ever could have imagined. We have reached a point that some have described as a new gilded age of concentrated wealth and power, ruled by bloated financial institutions and big tech.[5] Further, digital media and devices have crept deep into our lives with the rise of internet platforms and a reboot of the internet following the dot.com bust of 2000, bringing in ecommerce, social media, and a new business model now described as surveillance capitalism. These platforms, guided by artificial intelligence, have made enormous profits from monopolizing attention through their use of persuasive technologies. Some have cautioned that this system is exploiting human nature the way industrial capitalism exploited the natural world in the nineteenth and twentieth centuries.[6]

The changes to Seattle brought on by its tech boom have, indeed, been dramatic. Microsoft had been an established presence in the area since the early nineties and had already remade the east side of Lake Washington into a collection of affluent communities and suburbs. The center of Seattle, however, had yet to feel the blast of what was to come. Seattle's tech boom, led first by Microsoft (reined in by antitrust regulations in the late nineties) and then by Amazon.com (born in Seattle in 1994 as an online bookseller), brought tremendous new wealth, construction, and employment to the city, making it the fastest growing city in the United States from 2010-2020, with software developers surpassing retailers as the city's most common profession.[7] It also brought on *affluenza*: staggering wealth inequality and soaring housing costs, an exacerbated homelessness crisis, homogenization of once eclectic neighborhoods, overcrowding, and seemingly endless traffic gridlock.[8] All of this is occurring along with the existential threat of climate change in the background.[9]

This is not to say that there have not been benefits, and the digital age has brought on many marvels. I frequently enjoy humor, photos, and other content shared on social media, and the platforms have helped reconnect distant friends, initiate new relationships, and organize events quickly and easily. Quoting published and other quality online sources in academic papers is common now, and the ease of accessing published material through Google Books and Google Scholar, as well as having an obscure book delivered to my door overnight by Amazon.com, helped me meet deadlines in graduate school. Most of my sources for this project were online articles. You may have purchased this book on Amazon.com, and I am using my Facebook and Instagram accounts to promote it. Digital media also eliminate paper piles and their production (print newspapers have been disparaged as "dead tree productions" for many years now). I also recognize that the way we live, work, and take-in information has always been in flux due to changing market dynamics and new technologies, and the changes are often most visibly wrought in our cities. Even early forms of permanent writing were distrusted by some ancient cultures (the Celts, for example) who saw it as a threat to their prized skill of memorizing oral narratives.[10] In early modern Europe, the introduction of mass printing was viewed as the unfortunate end of handmade medieval book arts, and a dangerous tool giving voice to the masses that could be used to incite rebellion (which, of course, it did).[11]

However, nothing in the printed medium compares to the neurological barrage of digital media. Given the regular revelations about reckless nonfeasance in Silicon Valley, the monopolistic behaviors the tech giants, and firsthand experience of the negative effects of smartphones on relationships and social situations, it often seems that this technology has done more harm than good. The term "going viral" refers the frightening speed with which information, often misinformation, spreads online, and voices of hatred have exploited the free mouthpieces of social media to absurd degrees. The CEO of Amazon.com is now the one of the richest men in world history, while Washington State school libraries are being starved of staff and resources, and many are closing their doors altogether.[12] Amazon.com's effect on Seattle's used bookstores has been described as nothing short of "a slaughter."[13]

But the tide is turning. While the behemoth chain store Borders Books folded in 2011 and a struggling Barnes and Noble was sold to a hedge fund in June 2019, independent and used bookstores have enjoyed a small but steady comeback from 2009-2019.[14] With chain and big-box new book stores—chief rivals to independents in the eighties and nineties—crushed by the apex predator of ecommerce, "indie" populations were able to stabilize and begin to grow again in the niche left behind. Unlike the larger stores, small bookstores are an integral part of the ecology of street life and multi-use neighborhoods praised by Jane Jacobs as the components of a truly healthy city, an idea proven true again and again since the publication of her classic work, *The Death and Life of Great American Cities,* in 1961.[15] Some used bookstores have also weathered the transition by partnering with ecommerce merchants as third-party sellers, with very low prices that can compete with Amazon's.[16]

This project looks at bookstores from a range of Seattle's neighborhoods. It is not a "then and now" series, since only two of the stores photographed in 1999 remain open, and several places photographed in 2019 were open, but not visited, twenty years ago. It is not a "vanishing Seattle" documentary effort. The stores included here are doing very well and will likely thrive for many more years. In 2019, we visit Magus Books, Twice Sold Tales, BLMF Books, Lamplight Books, Arundel Books, the Globe Bookstore, Ophelia's Books, and Couth Buzzard Books. From 1999, we visit Beauty and the Books, Freedonia Books, and Recollection Books. Magus Books and Twice Sold Tales are covered most extensively, as they were visited in both 1999 and 2019. Many used bookstores have been omitted, because this was never intended as a catalogue or inventory-style documentation effort. I offer a small sample here to document the basic anatomy and behavior of these complex and fascinating urban organisms. This is also hardly the first, or last, comment on the value of books, reading, and bookstores, and many of the sentiments expressed here will already be familiar, having been noticed before in other bibliophile projects. My project, however, is a unique look at a critical moment in cultural history, with the Seattle situation as a proxy lens through which to consider the recent changes in our lives and cities.

It is, above all, a love note to books, print, and a thank-you note to the booksellers.

CHAPTER 1

TWICE SOLD TALES, CAPITOL HILL

1833 Harvard Avenue

There are no ordinary cats.
—Colette

Feel free to browse recklessly.
—Poster map of Twice Sold Tales bookstore

Twice Sold Tales, known to many as Seattle's coolest used bookstore, is one of the most recognizable and integral businesses in the Capitol Hill neighborhood. The Hill is a longtime haven of hipsters, artists, students, musicians, and LGBTQ community. The area is home to some of the grandest buildings in the city (art deco beauties dating back to the early twentieth century), Volunteer Park and Conservatory, Cornish College of the Arts, and Seattle Central Community College. Located just east of South Lake Union (the location of Amazonia), up a steep hill with a stunning view, the area has been hit hard by gentrification but stubbornly retains much of its character.

Jamie Lutton, the current and original owner of Twice Sold Tales, started selling books from a cart in the neighborhood's Broadway Market in 1987, following years of selling used books out of boxes on college campuses. She opened the flagship Twice Sold Tales store on Broadway and East John Street in 1990. By the late nineties, her store was well-loved for the many resident cats, interesting staff, and book selection that reflected the diversity of the Capitol Hill community. Twice Sold Tales would stay open until 2 a.m. during the week and all night on Fridays, offering discounts after midnight. Her store created a space for people who might not have anywhere else to go at these hours and kept reading affordable and accessible to all. The East John Street Twice Sold Tales, and the entire city block, are now a Soundlink Light Rail station, and condominium apartments now line Broadway in one and two-tier rows above what is left of the street-level retail stores.

Fortunately, Twice Sold Tales was not displaced too far and is currently located on Harvard Avenue East and East Denny Way, about a two-minute walk from its original location off Broadway. After the move to Harvard Avenue in 2008, the essence of Twice Sold Tales remains unchanged. Cats still rule the interior, and dinosaur motifs abound. The book selection, now expanded, still runs the gamut from sexuality studies to children's titles. In a 2008 essay by Doug Schwartz posted just after the move, Lutton reported on the changes.

> Clientele is a little older than it used to be and a little more residential, also not surprising since she's closer to more apartments and condos. She [Lutton] said she now sells fewer books about drugs and marijuana growing operations and is selling more mysteries, more books about birds and more science fiction. "I do my happy dance if someone wants to sell me science fiction titles," she said.
>
> Physically, the store is 50 percent larger than its predecessor and thus more titles fill the shelves, roughly 40,000 by Lutton's best guess. At one point this year she worked three straight months without a day off. Such is the life of an independent bookstore owner.
>
> She still relishes being a bookseller. Recently a customer came in and asked for a specific algebra textbook.

Jamie had the title at the counter within arms' reach and handed it over within seconds. It had been in the store for months but Lutton was just resorting it. Such moments of serendipity—not to mention a $50 sale—bring a smile to her face, and a stunned look on the face of the customer.

Lutton acknowledges that the Internet, Amazon's Kindle, and changing reading habits make the notion of running a brick-and-mortar used bookstore a far more precarious proposition than it used to be. But she's determined, and actually even nominally optimistic, about Twice Sold Tale's chances: "I'm having a good experience here. Business is not great but it's acceptable. I have a corps of regular customers who keep me open and I still have eight years left on my lease. I'm planning on staying."[17]

More than a decade after this interview, Jamie and the cats are still here. Lutton is an incredibly hardworking, fast-moving woman with a gentle smile and quick mind and keeps her store in her own way. She has been a bookselling powerhouse for over thirty years now, spinning off franchise Twice Sold Tales stores in downtown Seattle (now closed), Queen Anne (now closed), Fremont (a location that is now Ophelia's Books), and Ballard (formerly a University District location, and still open). One of her former employees, J. B. Johnson, now a bookseller himself, expressed that Lutton has not only created an ad hoc job corps for other booksellers, but she has "kept Seattle literate for thirty years" by with affordable books offered in a comfortable space. In July 2019, Lutton expressed no bitterness toward Amazon.com, but wishes its warehouse workers received better pay and treatment. While interacting with customers and staff, I overheard her offer intelligent, insightful comments on a wide range of books that passed through her hands, revealing just a glimpse of the depth of knowledge she has accrued during her bookselling career.

Hardy, Eleanor, Buster, and Lily are the current lords and ladies of Twice Sold Tales. Many other shelter cats, as many as seven at a time, have come and gone over the years; some found private homes if bookstore life did not suit them. The bookstore / library cat has a long history: cats have been preventing rodents from devouring paper collections since they guarded the papyrus scrolls in ancient Egypt. The bookstore cat phenomenon also reflects the natural symbiosis of cats, book places, and readers. As solitary ambush hunters, they are drawn to partially enclosed spaces that provide cover and allow them to survey their environment, such as paper bags and cardboard boxes, which used bookstores have in abundance. Cats are also natural climbers and fond of resting in high places. When the cat stand just isn't high enough, there are the bookshelves. For readers, a cat can be the perfect companion to the solitary act of reading, and cats know that a reader provides a warm lap or leg, a nice chin scratch, and a cuddle. Almost supernaturally sensitive to energy, cats seem to respond to the neuro-electricity involved in acts of concentration, giving rise to their habit of positioning themselves between a reader and her book.

Thanks to Jamie Lutton, both cats and books will have welcoming homes on Capitol Hill for many more years.

Twice Sold Tales, East John Street, 1999

Twice Sold Tales, Interior, East John Street, 1999

Twice Sold Tales, Interior with Cats and
Reader, East John Street, 1999

Twice Sold Tales, Interior with Reader on Carnation Dairy Crate, East John Street, 1999

Twice Sold Tales, Interior with Book Browsers, East John Street, 1999

Twice Sold Tales, Exterior Entrance, Harvard Avenue, 1999

Twice Sold Tales, Exterior, Harvard Avenue, 2019

Jamie Lutton at Twice Sold Tales, 2019

Hardy, Twice Sold Tales, 2019

Buster, Twice Sold Tales, 2019

Eleanor and Browser, Twice Sold Tales, 2019

Lily, Twice Sold Tales, 2019

Lily, Twice Sold Tales, 2019

Twice Sold Tales, Book Cart from Everett School District, 2019

Twice Sold Tales, Rubbing of Shakespeare's Grave, 2019

Twice Sold Tales, Reader on Carnation Dairy Crate, 2019

Twice Sold Tales, Selected Subjects, 2019

CHAPTER 2

MAGUS BOOKS, UNIVERSITY DISTRICT

1408 NE Forty-Second Street

Books are the only true magic.
—Alice Hoffman

Magus Books is tucked inside a three-story, ivy-covered 1903 building, originally a Post Office, near the northwest corner of the University of Washington campus between Fifteenth Avenue Northeast and University Way ("the Ave"). The surrounding area was rezoned in 2017 to allow for construction of twenty- and thirty-story buildings, but a Save the Ave movement has kept a pedestrian-oriented stretch of small businesses, long the heart of off-campus life for UW students and faculty, from the encroachment. Many retail businesses, coffee shops, and independent restaurants I remember from my student years in the late nineties are long gone, replaced mostly by banks, chain restaurants, and take-out noodle shops. Magus, however, is still thriving. Now owned and operated by Chris Weimer and Hannah McElroy, the store has had several previous lives: a run as the radical Puss 'n' Books, then the Id Bookstore in the sixties and early seventies, eventually christened Magus (from a root word for magic or royalty) when it was purchased by Dave Bell in 1978. It is one of the last used bookstores still operating in the University District, and the only one selling used books exclusively.

On a bright, sunny day in July 2019, the door to Magus was propped open with a box to let fresh air and customers drift in. Its interior has not changed at all in twenty years. The space strikes just the right blend of order and entropy, with stacks and escarpments of books, the subjects mixing and mingling while waiting to be shelved. University students and professors bring in many specialized and academic texts, but popular fiction, children's books, and even sheet music are also well represented. The collection of art books has always been particularly strong. Magus is suffused with a pleasant smell of paper bags, cardboard boxes, coffee and baked goods from Café Allegro (Seattle's original espresso bar) around the corner, and a quiet murmur of business and casual conversations. Heading up the counter is a welcoming bookseller, Hallie, brimming with intelligence. The bookshelves and walls are galleries of quotes, humor, and other print ephemera, including a diagrammatic chart of world history, a poster of nasturtiums, and bibliophile humor. Being in Magus feels like being in the cozy home of a friend who has spent her life reading, traveling, cooking, studying art and more, and has curated her experiences along the way in books, art cards, posters, and other varied on paper.

Employees often come from the ranks of University of Washington students, many of them cutting their literary teeth before moving on to journalism, publishing, libraries, teaching, and other pursuits. In his 2013 article "Seattle's Disappearing Bookstores," magazine journalist Charles Fischer recalls some of his time working at Magus.

> While I was in graduate school in the '90s, I worked as a clerk at Magus Books in the University District—a neighborhood that has consistently defied gentrification. Magus is arguably one of the best bookshops in the city. Much of its spirit goes back to Dave Bell, who bought it in the 1970s and was its longest and most formative owner, giving the store its distinct shape and personality. An outspoken advocate for civil liberties, the late owner kept a brand-new copy of *The Anarchist Cookbook,* along with psychedelic mushroom kits, in the locked

display case in the front of the store. Though Bell had a science background, he made a point of hiring liberal arts people, many working toward advanced degrees or already with them. Rhodes scholars worked side by side with graduate students in English and philosophy.

A day spent in Magus was a day spent in the best class you ever had in college—I remember talking about the pattern of human carelessness in *The Great Gatsby* with Dave Heller, who now teaches philosophy at Seattle University, and having Bill Kiesel, now publisher and editor of Ouroboros Press, break down the dialectical gymnastics behind *Malleus Maleficarum*, a medieval treatise on witches. Hanging out in Magus was like hanging out with the knowledgeable and quirky clerks in [the movie] *High Fidelity*. Perhaps the only reason Hollywood has never made a hit movie about used bookstores is they don't come with a soundtrack. ...

It's not just the books and the clerks who create the distinct culture of the used bookstore; the stacks attract customers straight out of Dickens. Among my favorites were the one-armed man who visited daily, always whistling an enigmatic tune; and the neurotic, down-on-his-heels anthropology adjunct who would pace the store rearranging the stacks and leave without making a purchase. The oddest, however, was the customer who only came into the store on Husky football days and who would ask whomever was working the cash register where the books on sex and Nazis were located. He then would go to their respective aisles, pull a half-dozen of each off the shelf, open and spread them on the floor, where he would lie down and caress their pages like a world-weary voluptuary at an orgy of Nero.[18]

While browsing the stacks, I found autographed copies of *The Valley of Horses* by Jean M. Auel, skimmed a handbook on the philosophy of Karl Popper with a gift receipt still inside, and almost without realizing it, became so absorbed in Margaret Atwood's *Cat's Eye* that I lost track of time. My instinct was to apologize to a member of the staff for staying too long, and her friendly response was "Oh, that's fine. I hate it when people just come and go and don't read anything. What a shame." Later the same day, I saw a post by woman who took her adolescent daughter to Magus (after overcoming much resistance) and posted the results on the store's Facebook page. "Complained bigly but ended up engrossed. These places are magic."[19]

Two University District bookstores along the Ave, both now closed, Recollection Used Books and Beauty and the Books, were also unique specimens of the used bookstore and quite different in aesthetic, collections, and ambience. Recollection Fine Used Books, once located on 4519 University Way, featured a collection strong in twentieth-century history and literature, in particular books on the Vietnam War, radicalism, labor and beat literature, gender, and African American studies. Recollection also sold collectibles including autographed copies and first editions. The store frequently displayed the art of one of the booksellers, James Koehnline, who remains a productive working artist specializing in digital media. This location is now a smoke shop.

Beauty and the Books, owned by the late Richard B. Leffel (1934–2011), occupied an Easter egg-colored Victorian building on 4213 University Way for over three decades. It was known for its reader-friendly couches and over 150,000 eclectic titles as well as used tapes, CDs, videos, autographed books, photos, and artwork. According to his obituary in *The Seattle Times,* Leffel passed in February 2011, asleep with a book on his chest. During his life, he was "unfailingly generous, a refuge for many and an unmatched storyteller and lover of literature."[20] The former home of Beauty and the Books now houses a Subway sandwich shop and a vacant space and is currently a project of the Save the Ave preservation movement.

Magus Books, Interior Stacks, 1999

Magus Books, Bookseller, 1999

Magus Books, Interior Stacks, continued, 1999

Magus Books, Exterior, 2019

Magus Books, Iconic Store Sign, 2019

Magus Books, Interior, Keep the U District Unique, 2019

Magus Books, Ephemera: Hell's Bibliophiles, 2019

Magus Books, Ephemera II, 2019

Magus Books, Interior Stacks Forever, 2019

Magus Books, Original Puss 'N Books store sign, 2019

Magus Books, Street View with New Construction, 2019

University District Bookstores, now closed.

Recollection Used Books, Exterior Entrance, University Way, 1999

Recollection Used Books, Bookseller James Koehnline, 1999

Recollection Used Books, Bookseller's Desk, 1999

Beauty and the Books, Interior, 1999

Beauty and the Books, Reader, 1999

Beauty and the Books, Bookseller and Store
President David Clumper, 1999

CHAPTER 3

BLMF BOOKS AND LAMPLIGHT BOOKS, PIKE PLACE MARKET

```
1501 Pike Place, 1514 Pike Place
```

The presence of books acquired produces such an ecstasy that the buying of more books than one can read is nothing less than the soul reaching towards infinity.
—A. Edward Newton

A room without books is like a body without a soul.
—Cicero

In the lower terraces of Pike Place Market on Seattle's downtown waterfront hill, under the throngs of tourists, buckets of flowers, seafood, and tossed fish, you will find dim corridors brightened up by independent bookstores and other small-scale retailers. BLMF Books: A Literary Saloon is owned and operated by J. B. Johnson. While saloon simply means "public place," BLMF does feel like the bookstore version of your favorite hang out. Johnson has been in the book business since the nineties, first as a Jamie Lutton disciple managing a downtown Twice Sold Tales, then moving on to open BLMF Books in 1996 when a Pike Place Market location became available. What he thought would be a short-term gig has now lasted over twenty years, and business is not slowing down.

BLMF takes its name from a comment once dropped to J. B. about the size of his at-home book collection. "Man, you have books like a motherf----r." Indeed, at BLMF, the books create the space. Paperbacks and hardbacks line the walls from floor to ceiling, fill windows and boxes, create islands of interesting geometry, spine-line mosaic patterns, and form vertical columns and horizontal rows until they can go no farther. About half of these books come from in-store sales and trades, while many more are found by Johnson himself at yard sales, estate sales, thrift stores, and even the occasional abandoned storage unit (when a tip arrives). Titles are wildly eclectic, and his fiction collection is huge.

A location in the world-famous Pike Place Market brings a steady flow of walk-in customers, and there is no online business. The people, Johnson says, are both "the best and worst part of the job." Some are befuddled tourists swinging selfie-sticks, dripping ice cream on the floor and pawing through books with sticky food fingers, while many others are thoughtful, excited browsers and buyers. Johnson, himself a world traveler with an impressive international photo collage in his store, notes that the transnational and international visitors he receives give insight into the interests and reading habits of people outside his own community. Some purchases are predictable, but with a twist. For example, a teenage girl from Japan was thrilled to buy her own complete set of the Twilight Saga *in Seattle*. While visiting BLMF, I met and chatted with a couple from Brooklyn. One woman described the "warmth" she feels upon entering a bookstore and the connection she experiences to her late mother when reading her favorite books. I left the store feeling delighted with my finds: five books of Mary Oliver's poetry and *The History of the Book in 100 Books: From Egpyt to Ebook*, by Roderick Cave and Sara Ayad, a summary I had been hoping to find *someday* and did not know had already been written until my visit to BLMF.

One floor up, but still below street level, the golden glow of Lamplight Books draws you into its small, tidy space of bookshelves, yellow walls, and red trim. Lamplight Books was opened in 2003 by an Italian woman, Lidia Icardi, who designed and maximized her small space. She created a small but carefully selected collection and decorated the store with antique lamps sourced from Seattle thrift stores. When Icardi returned to Italy in 2014, one of her employees, Joe Fridlund, purchased the store twenty years "to the day" after his arrival in Seattle. Before acquiring Lamplight, Fridlund also held positions at BLMF Books, Spine & Crown on Capitol Hill (now closed), and Jive Time Records in Freemont.

Fridlund says that maintaining the small, carefully curated book collection is a "constant struggle" that sometimes keeps him up at night. "Keeping the shelves filled with interesting, quality books is the biggest challenge we have, but somehow, a new collection always seems to present itself," he says.

Philosophy, poetry, and literature in translation are particularly strong areas within Lamplight. The payoff for all the hard work, Fridland says, is when customers find a book they have wanted for a long time but couldn't find elsewhere. Like at BLMF, all of Lamplight's business comes from walk-in customers. Fridlund also enjoys the daily contact with international visitors. "Many people have lost the small independent shops in the places they live, and they are always so excited to find a real bookshop. Others have bookstores back home, but they don't have the same eclectic selection that we offer," he comments. "People talk about the end, but I see a long future for books. The printed page is one of the greatest technologies ever invented, and I think it will be around for a long, long time." I found a copy of Stephen King's *Misery* with the same cover art as the edition I read many years ago, momentarily taking me back to my King-obsessed adolescent years. The next exciting and completely unexpected find was a 1926 Chicago Field Museum anthropology leaflet, "Ostrich Egg-Shell Cups of Ancient Mesopotamia and the Ostrich in Ancient and Modern Times."

Two booksellers, very different but equally wonderful, have no trouble drawing in urban tourists in a venue more famous for food and flowers. While tourism accounts for much of its business, BLMF and Lamplight also maintain a devoted local customer base, reflected in the glowing online reviews praising the owners' expertise, the low book prices, and the fun of visiting their stores. Charisma, it seems, often outweighs the convenience of the click.

BLMF Books: A Literary Saloon, Pike Place Market, Exterior Entrance, 2019

BLMF Books, Bookseller and Owner J.B. Johnson, 2019

BLMF Books, J. B. Johnson's Travel Wall (detail), 2019.

BLMF Books, Book Wall, 2019

BLMF Books, Child Browsing, 2019

Lamplight Books, Exterior Entrance, 2019

Lamplight Books, Interior, 2019

Lamplight Books, Lamp, 2019

CHAPTER 4

THE GLOBE AND ARUNDEL BOOKS, PIONEER SQUARE

218 and 212 First Avenue South

Oh, I just want what we all want: a comfortable couch, a nice beverage, a weekend of no distractions, and a book that will stop time, lift me out of my quotidian existence, and alter my thinking forever.
—Elizabeth Gilbert

Just off Seattle's waterfront is the historic Pioneer Square, one of the city's oldest neighborhoods with a layout and infrastructure that have changed little since the turn-of-the century Klondike gold rush that first generated the area. The neighborhood is frequented by tourists but is also dense with office space, residential apartment buildings, art galleries and a host of artists' lofts. Seattle's two large professional sports stadiums reside in an open sprawl just a few blocks to the south, drawing sports fans by the tens of thousands on game days. In the heart of the square, a Neo-Romanesque building houses two independent bookstores, Arundel Books and the Globe. Ars Obscura, a traditional book binding and restoration business continuing a 500-year-old European trade, occupies the building's lower level.

The Globe, owned by John and Carolyn Siscoe, has been in business since 1978, starting as two small bookstores in the University District and downtown. John Siscoe, a warm, welcoming man, speaks fondly of his forty years in the bookselling business and is optimistic about the future of bookstores. He notes that books are never really owned—they are "stewarded"—and his successful, decades-long used book business demonstrates this. Like the stores in Pike Place Market, the Globe serves walk-in customers only, drawing in both tourists and locals; there is no online business. In recent years, Siscoe reports, sales have actually improved, and he believes that many young people have already grown tired of screens and ebooks. His observation is accurate: sales of ebooks have steadily fallen for the past three years, while hardback and paperback purchases have increased.[21] I purchased a Barnes and Noble Nook in 2013, and it never quite found a place in my home, migrating from the miscellaneous electronics bin to the bookshelves and then back to a box when I grew tired of looking at the cord tangle. I only ever read two ebooks. I missed cover art, marking and folding pages, and passing a finished book along to a friend. Just as music lovers enjoy the art, notes, and "needle-on-the-record" experience of vinyl, many readers relish the pleasurable visual and tactile stimuli that comes with print.

The Globe is a delightful jumble: open boxes stacked behind the bookshelves, hand-made art cards, delightfully incongruous titles placed side by side, the presence of cats suggested by cards and photos, and gorgeous posters of northwest trees and wildflowers. There are a large number of titles on Seattle along with northwest-themed posters and other paper products that are popular with both tourists and locals. In the nineties, the University District store's student-oriented collection was especially strong in classics, Eastern and Western philosophy, and all eras of world literature. Upstairs, a nice reading chair covered in a crochet blanket supports a collection of books about fiber arts. Siscoe was delighted by my purchase of a large Saul Steinberg collection, and we chatted about the artist for several minutes before he returned to his work. Nearing retirement, Siscoe is no longer actively acquiring books for the Globe and operates on a month-to-month lease.

While browsing in the stacks and, later, going over the photographs of the store, the word *semiotics* kept appearing on books and note cards. Semiotics, the study of how meaning is derived from images and marks, a continuum beginning with an image and culminating in writing, reminds us of how remarkable the mental phenomenon really is.[22] It is interesting to notice where the mind goes when scanning the photographs containing bold titles, images without words, and combinations of words and images: where do the images, letters, and words take you? How did the pathways emerge, and how were they forged? Do they change as you move from image to image? Where do you pause the longest?

Arundel Books is one door away. Arundel was founded in 1984 by Phil Bevis, originally in Los Angeles as a publisher and online bookseller. His mission is to "reflect and enhance the community in which he lives and works," and the multi-faceted business demonstrates the range of activities involved in bookselling culture. His Pioneer Square store opened in 1995, selling new, used, and rare books. The LA store has now been closed for twenty-seven years. Arundel is a retail space, an online bookstore, and partner to another independent publisher, Chatwin Press. Arundel's 1,000-square-foot-store holds thousands of volumes of art and poetry along with fiction, children's titles, art and design, photography, and hard sciences, with prices ranging from a few dollars for a used book to many thousands of dollars for a collector's item. It is also a gallery space, and the July 2019 exhibit featured a colorful collection of autographed prints, *Fishes of the Salish Sea*, by Joseph Tomelleri. Bevis mentions that on the best days at Arundel Books,

> People come in from all over, from all walks of life, with all interests. They could be from across the street, China, or Peru. They can be rich or poor, tall or short, young or old. Their interests run the gamut from poetry to pirates, to particle physics and pop-up books. What

makes it fun is that so many of them are truly *excited* to find a bookstore. It makes what we do feel hip and cool.

Arundel has succeeded, he says, by adapting to changing customer preferences and habits.

In a dynamic time, Bevis only looks ahead about one year when planning his next business move. He has previously spoken of a desire to bring more independent booksellers to the area.[23] During his early years in LA, he had worked on "bookseller's row," a collection of twenty-two bookstores in a four-block section of the city. Bookselling, both Bevis and Siscoe report, is a business that thrives in concentration. Siscoe sends customers right next door to Arundel if they don't find what they are looking for at his store, and he recalls that business in the University District was best when there were more stores along University Way. Many of the world's oldest cities also have or once possessed their own bookseller's row. Al-Mutanabi street in Baghdad, Iraq, the city's intellectual and literary hub since the 8th century, welcomed 22-year old Ruqaya Fawziya as its first female bookseller in 2015.[24]

Bevis echoes the always appreciated observation that bookstores "provide a place for people to discover new passions, support old ones, and meet other people who love books." Indeed, one minute into a chat with Arundel's bookseller and gallery curator Tori Champion, we discovered that we are both in the same field: she was preparing for her first term of graduate studies in art history at the University of Washington. This was another reminder of the kind of fun and fortuitous encounter that only place can engender.

Also pictured is Freedonia Books, from 1999. Freedonia Books closed its doors on First Avenue in 2000 due to an increase in the downtown rents, after six years as a brick-and-mortar business. Its online bookstore, based on Bainbridge Island across the sound from Seattle, aimed to retain the eclectic book selection of the original store. They also incorporated a bookstore cat on a webcam.

Home of The Globe Bookstore and Arundel Books, First Avenue, 2019

Approaching The Globe Bookstore, First Avenue, 2019.

John Siscoe, Owner and Bookseller, The Globe Bookstore, 2019

The Globe, Books and Cards, 2019

The Globe, Art Cards, 2019

The Globe, Reader, 2019

The Globe, Mary Oliver, 2019

Arundel Books, Exterior Entrance, First Avenue, 2019

Arundel Books, Interior, 2019

Bookseller Tori Champion, Arundel Books, 2019

Arundel Books, Balzac Titles, 2019

Downtown / Pioneer Square Bookstores, now closed:

Freedonia Books, First Avenue, Child Browsing, 1999

Freedonia Books, Interior, 1999

CHAPTER 5

OPHELIA'S BOOKS, FREMONT

3504 Fremont Avenue North

A beggar's book out-worths a noble's blood.
—Shakespeare

Ophelia's Books, on Fremont Avenue north, is located in the center of the universe (also known as Seattle's Fremont neighborhood). Still a hub of bohemian life, Fremont is located on the north side of the ship canal connecting the Salish Sea with Lake Union, just a short distance from downtown and South Lake Union. It is a longtime nexus of independent businesses, restaurants, small homes and apartments, gardens, and free spirit living. The annual Fremont Solstice Parade draws out body-painted revelers, and the neighborhood is home to outdoor sculptures including a painted rocket ship, an authentic Soviet statue of Lenin imported after the fall of the USSR, and an enormous troll carved beneath a bridge overpass. The area has also attracted many from the tech workforce, and while the two cultures coexist, the changing demographic has put considerable pressure on longtime residents.[25] A local satirical newspaper, *The Needling: Seattle's Only Real Fake News*, "reported" in 2018 that the beloved Fremont Troll was priced out of Fremont and had to relocate to a more affordable area.[26] Fortunately, small independent wonders like Ophelia's Books remain in the heart of the neighborhood.

Ophelia's Books got its start in 1996 as a franchise of Twice Sold Tales, first headed up by Lisa Perry. Perry had worked in the original Twice Sold Tales location on Capitol Hill for four years before opening the location in Fremont. In 2000, she created her own place in the manner of her favorite bookstores in the United Kingdom, choosing the name Ophelia's Books in honor of the bookstore's resident cat. The current owner, Jill Levine, also a bookkeeper, acquired the store (with cats) in 2011 after fourteen years as a loyal customer.

When discussing the business, Levine's conversation reveals some of the fallout Fremont residents feel in the blast zone of big tech. Used bookstores, Levine says, are where you "have a chance to let a book find you, in sharp contrast to the point and search mechanism of online shopping." She alludes to one of the pitfalls of online activity: *filter bubbles*, the phenomenon in which algorithms generate search results that align with what a browser has already found, a self-perpetuating loop that discourages exposure to new ideas.[27] Thus, Levine notes, Amazon has a "stranglehold" on what people are actually reading as well as the sale of books. The quickly rotating chance stock of used bookstores, however, has the opposite effect. Ophelia's Books has also sold books online since 1997, but Levine stresses that online selling is a completely distinct process and skill set.

She has also witnessed, with dismay, the steady dwindling of Seattle bookstores, from five or more in a neighborhood to only one or none at all. Addressing the role of bookstores in a community, Levine comments:

> Ten years ago, I went to a talk that stressed the importance of the bookshop as a place where people converge and exchange ideas, increasingly necessary in a technology-oriented world. This is even more true today. But our existence is only half the equation.
>
> The other half is people showing up with the intent to use this tool to its greatest advantage.

And while people still love the idea of used bookstores—their collections, the prices written in pencil inside the books, the cats—her query is that it might be just the *idea* that they love. Nevertheless, Levine still enjoys the day-to-day experience of running the store and notes that "enthusiastic, book-loving people come to Ophelia's every day. They love the atmosphere. They browse and find books they are excited about. They talk to the cat."

Located next door to Jive Time Records, a vintage vinyl record store, Ophelia's Books brightens up Fremont Avenue with a red neon sign and an oversize, book-shaped sign board, a visual that fits nicely with the outdoor sculpture tradition in the neighborhood. Inside, the small space is divided into three stories, complete with a spiral staircase to the lowest level, headed up by a London Underground symbol. While eclectic, the interior strikes a note of midcentury modern chic, featuring an aquamarine, sparkle-vinyl reading couch, rows of pulp fiction, and fifties paperback cover art on wall display. An upper nook houses a comfortable reading area, a papier-mâché cat, and some relics from a library. All throughout the store, unique items—from an old-fashioned mobile to a framed Arabic ink inscription on decorated paper—add further interest and character. The book selection is as wide and varied as any, and the Eastern religion and philosophy shelves appeared to be particularly strong. I was delighted to find a copy of *McElligot's Pool*, by Dr. Seuss, a childhood favorite I had completely forgotten until this visit.

It found me.

Ophelia's Books, Exterior Entrance, Freemont Avenue North, 2019

Jill Levine at Ophelia's Books, 2019

Ophelia's Books, Interior Decor, 2019

Ophelia's Books, Front Window, 2019

Ophelia's Books, Vintage Paperbacks, 2019

Ophelia's Books, Spiral Staircase to Lower Level, 2019

Twice Sold Tales, Fremont Avenue North
(now Ophelia's Books), 1999

CHAPTER 6

COUTH BUZZARD BOOKS, GREENWOOD

8310 Greenwood Avenue North

You think your pain and your heartbreak are unprecedented in the history of the world, but then you read.
—James Baldwin

Far from the downtown hustle is the quiet Seattle neighborhood of Greenwood, home to Couth Buzzard Books on Greenwood Avenue. Greenwood is one of Seattle's single-family-home neighborhoods cut through with a small avenue of restaurants, coffee shops and retailers. Couth Buzzard Books has maintained a business in the neighborhood for twenty-five years and celebrated its tenth anniversary in its current location on 2019. The unusual name comes from the original owners who had envisioned a cafe and bookstore with a humorous, two-word title similar to those they had seen in the United Kingdom, such as the Flying Pig. Using the initials for *café* and *bookstore*, they coined the name *Couth Buzzard*.

The kindly Theo Dzielak took ownership of the store in 2009, finally adding the long-desired café and expanding the store to include a gathering space and performance venue. Dzielak, a musician trained in jazz, flute, and music of the Middle East, knew that the bookstore would need to adapt to survive in the twenty-first century. While the books, 80 percent of which are used, are still the heart of the store,

Couth Buzzard has also succeeded as a local community center. It is known and appreciated throughout the city for its jazz scene, four-day jazz festival, and Wednesday night open mic sessions welcoming everyone from poets to comedians. A packed schedule of daily meetups includes yoga, Buddhist studies, drumming, mindfulness workshops, Spanish, Gaelic, Café Français, Celtic Jams, acoustic nights, news reviews, Zumba, watercolor, board games, Girl Scout meetings, book clubs, and more. On my visit in July 2019, I enjoyed a refreshing meal at its bar-style cafe while chatting with Theo.

Just a few dollars bought two paperbacks (one with an address sticker still inside) and a children's book, *Castle of Books*. Inside *Castle* was the inscription, "To Emmett and his Papa David, who loves books like you do. Love, Nana." From the selection of Couth Buzzard's new books, I completed a set of slim, three-by-five-inch paperback *How To* books by the Zen teacher Thich Nhat Hanh. *How to Love, How to Sit, How to Fight, How to Eat, How to Walk,* and *How to Relax* communicate simple tools for alleviating suffering and increasing joy every day. My collection began with the purchase of *How to Love* at Arundel Books just a few days earlier.

A woman seated nearby was practicing the Coast Salish art of cedar weaving, looking very peaceful and content in the afternoon summer sun streaming into the store. A man read quietly by himself at the bar, choosing to be alone in proximity to other people. The bookstore as a café and community center—occasionally also a bar— has been a successful formula at Couth Buzzard and in other used and new bookstores in Seattle (particularly the aptly-named Third Place Books, which now has three locations in Lake Forest Park, Ravenna, and Seward Park) and across the country, reinforcing the importance of the place away from home and work where the magic of connection and community can take place. The stated mission of Couth Buzzard is to "build community: one book, one cup, one note at a time." A more important endeavor is difficult to imagine.

Couth Buzzard Books, Entrance on Greenwood Avenue, 2019

Theo Dzeilak at Couth Buzzard's Cafe Buono, 2019

Couth Buzzard, Interior, 2019

Posters for Couth Buzzard Jazz Festival, 2019

Couth Buzzard, Interior Artwork, 2019

Couth Buzzard, Children's Nook, 2019

CONCLUSION

A book is a machine to think with.
—Ivor A. Richards

We are running an uncontrolled evolutionary experiment, and the results so far are terrifying.
—Roger McNamee

2020 is a critical moment for humanity, and we do have a choice about how we want to live. The ultimate fate of used bookstores will reflect the values that endure in the next decades, as cities struggle to rebalance while coping with dramatic ecological changes. While used bookstores alone are surely not enough to save us from ourselves, we can all benefit by spending less time with our tech toys and more time in real venues with other people and books.

TECH TROUBLES

It doesn't take a luddite to notice that the years 2016–2019 revealed some truly corrosive effects of big tech and the toxicity of social media. Casualties include privacy and data security, the verity and quality of the information we consume, mental health and well-being, harmony in interpersonal relations, and even the integrity of our democracy.[28] When misused, social media platforms have brought on perils (e.g., targeted disinformation leading to horrific incited violence) in addition to less extreme but still troubling afflictions (e.g., distracted parenting, cyberbullying, mood shattering experiences). There is never a "last page" online or in the stories and feeds of social media sites, and the platforms are designed to keep you there, keep you returning, and revealing as much as possible about your preferences and habits to the data collection machines. From 2017 to 2019, scrutiny and pressure have squeezed apologies, and even steep fines, from some of the biggest players in the game of collecting and monetizing personal data (let us call a spade a spade), but at the time of this writing, nothing has essentially changed. In 2016, internet addiction disorder was considered the number one health problem in China.[29] This situation resembles a technological panopticon, a prison in which we are constantly viewed from without.

Those of us who grew up without the internet and smartphones fondly remember when we walked to the library and the bookstore to get a book, and called friends to chat or meet up instead of defaulting to social media when we craved connection. Many have realized, to our dismay, that our smartphones are the first thing we touch in the morning and the last thing we touch at night. Simply setting up the morning alarm on the smartphone can easily turn into checking email and scrolling through pictures, and what was once an hour or two of nighttime reading can quickly be usurped by screen time, with all its emotional triggers and other sleep-interrupting side effects.

Deep reading has taken a hit. Online articles tend to be shorter than those in print and subject to pop-ups, banner ads, and links within the text that pull you to another topic before finishing even one short essay. Many advertisements arrive camouflaged as articles, with the disclaimer "sponsored content" just barely appearing above their headlines. Further, when local print newspapers disappear, so does their oversight of local affairs, and the online journalism that takes their place does not always measure up to the standards of print as shorter, breezier articles can better compete for clicks, reposts, and retweets, and thus generate more ad revenue.[30] Sound bites from Twitter now frequently replace newspaper articles as sources for the evening news reports. Print archives, while ponderous, cannot be deleted with a click and/or be easily manipulated to serve whoever is currently in power. In our personal lives, many of us miss letters, postcards, and other ways of connecting off the screen.

THE READING REMEDY

Books and bookstores will have a bright future as long as today's children have a chance to enjoy them. Paleolithic cave paintings can attest that humans have been telling stories with pictures since before we could grow our own food; indeed, it is part of what makes us Homo Sapiens.[31] Thus, it is no surprise that children are naturally drawn to stories and picture books when given the opportunity to read and be read to. Nevertheless, story time now faces stiff competition from electronics both at home and in the classroom with "educational technology"—a $60 billion business as of 2016.[32]

Parents, educators, and psychologists have been concerned about technology's effects on children since television arrived, while common sense and observation also raise many red flags about the harmful effects of too much tech. In contrast, modern neuroscience confirms that reading picture books with your child helps the brain develop in the areas of concentration, attention, emotional regulation and memory in ways that screen time does not.

> Animation of the sort that children might see on a TV screen or tablet is "too hot." There is just too much going on, too quickly, for the children to be able to participate in what they were seeing. Small children's brains have no difficulty registering bright, fast-moving images, as experience teaches and MRI scanning confirms, but the giddy shock and awe of animation doesn't give them time to exercise their deeper cognitive faculties.
>
> Just as Goldilocks sighs with relief when she takes a spoonful from the third bowl of porridge and finds that it is "just right," so a small child can relax into

the experience of being read a picture book. There is a bit of pleasurable challenge in making sense of what s/he's seeing and hearing. There is time to reflect on the story and to see its reverberations in their own lives. The collaborative engagement that a child brings to the experience is so vital and productive that reading aloud "stimulates optimal patterns of brain development," as a 2014 paper from the American Academy of Pediatrics put it, strengthening the neural connections that will enable a child to process more difficult and complex stories as s/he gets older.[33]

Cognitive skills are far from the only positive benefits that come from reading. Compassion and kindness can be learned through simple stories as children empathize with the experiences related in the narratives; this is not always the case for action-packed cartoons, and certainly not video games that are designed to create addictive adrenaline and dopamine rushes. Stories can gently convey life lessons and comfort in difficult situations, such as the death of pet, challenges in school and among peers, or simply the first lost tooth. Best of all are the moments of shared warmth and contact created by story time.

Like the seductive, efficient "IT" in Madeleine L'Engle's classic *A Wrinkle in Time*, the entity that ultimately consumed what it attracted, the digital world cannot provide the love, warmth, and real human connection that are essential to our well-being. It is no small irony that IT is now the widely-used acronym for Information Technology. We must be diligent in keeping books and reading in our children's lives. The stakes are simply too high.

THE BEAUTY OF THE USED BOOKSTORE

In sum, used books and bookstores remind us that not everything has to be fast and new to be valuable, as the magic of a book's content is not diminished by age, a tattered cover, written marks, or coffee stains on its pages. Knowing that the book could still be of value, it was passed along, linking strangers' lives in the process. The experiences of bookstore owners—how they curate their stores, the personal styles that suffuse each space, and the experiences of their booksellers and patrons—attest to the human as well as the literary narratives and knowledge that each bookstore encapsulates. Bookstores—and the literacy, community, and human connection they engender—might be one way to hold on to some of the best parts of our cities and societies in the coming decades. I extend my admiration to the booksellers who have weathered a challenging time, and I hope that this small project of gratitude reminds them of the positive legacy their lives and work will leave behind.

APPENDIX

A Very Brief Overview of Seattle History

Pacific Northwest people have always been exceptionally resilient and resourceful. People have lived in the region for thousands of years following the dissolution of the region's Cordilleran Glacier, some 10,000 years ago. Coast Salish culture groups such as the Suquamish (People of the Clear Salt Water) thrived on the sea and forest, especially the cedar tree, out of which they made homes, canoes, clothing, tools, baskets, medicine, masks, and large-scale carvings that have become icons of the region and its varied indigenous cultures.[34] Central Puget Sound was one of the most densely populated areas of North America in the precontact period, and native people once covered the land "as the waves of a wind-ruffled sea cover its shell-paved floor."[35] *Seattle* is the anglicized version of the name *Sealth*, in honor of Chief Sealth of the Suquamish and Duwamish tribes.

The history of Euro-American settlement in Seattle during the latter half of the nineteenth century follows the familiar trajectory of eighteenth-century explorers, fur trappers, missionaries, pioneers, homesteaders, and upstarts gradually displacing the native population and extracting local resources. Seattle, officially founded in 1851 and incorporated into Washington Territory in 1869, was one of many mill towns in the Puget Sound region that provided lumber for the surrounding communities and San Francisco, a boom industry that marked the end of Puget Sound's ancient forests. Life in the region was challenging even by nineteenth-century standards. Thick forests made road building difficult, and schoolchildren often traveled by boat to attend school, risking their lives battling strong tides and unpredictable weather.

The discovery of coal at the shores of Lake Washington (and San Francisco's endless demand) kept Seattle growing explosively into the 1880s, with an economy further supported by shipbuilding, wholesale trade, fishing, shipping, and the completion of the Northern Pacific Railroad forty miles to the south. An extensive fire in 1889 paused the growth only briefly, as Seattle was rebuilt with much grander brick and steel buildings on widened, improved streets and a new waterfront protected by a fire department and other municipal services. After another lull in the 1890s, Seattle boomed again as a launching point for prospectors headed into the 1897 Klondike gold rush in Alaska and the Canadian Yukon Territory, giving rise to Pioneer Square, a neighborhood of monumental stone buildings that remain landmarks today.

The early twentieth century saw several more boom-and-bust cycles accompanying national events, wars, recessions, and other social changes. The completion of two more transcontinental railroads and ongoing shipping relations with Asia brought in a more diverse population. The Denny Regrade, a project lasting from 1903 to 1916, leveled the 16 million cubic yards of dirt on Denny Hill, mostly by large blasts of water, and greatly expanded the downtown business district.[36] The resulting area is still known as *the regrade* by hard-core Seattleites. The Olmstead brothers, founders of landscape architecture in the United States and the firm behind New York City's Central Park and Prospect Park, developed a park and greenbelt system from 1903 to 1937 that "few cities could or can match."[37] The Seattle Symphony was founded in 1903. Seattle was celebrated as the center of the north Pacific rim in 1909's Alaska-Pacific-Yukon World's Fair. The two World Wars amplified shipbuilding and airplane manufacturing, giving rise to the Boeing Corporation. A world's fair in 1962 bequeathed the Seattle Space Needle, the Seattle Center (a site for recreation, education, food, retail, and cultural festivals), and the famous Monorail, which revived a downtown district hit hard by the rise of car culture and white flight to the suburbs.

From the 1950s to the present day economic vicissitudes have continued to run their course. One low point came with a national recession in 1971 that hit Boeing so hard that a billboard next to Sea Tac airport read, "Will the last person leaving Seattle please turn out the lights?" The city bounced back in the 1980s, and the tech boom arrived shortly thereafter. In spite of economic ups and downs, or perhaps because of them, independent arts and music have been a central part of city life in events such as the Seattle Folklife Festival, now in its forty-eighth year, and the international Bumbershoot Music Festival, held in the Seattle Center every Labor Day weekend since 1971. While there have always been affluent neighborhoods, most of the city was built as relatively modest, single-family, wood homes with yards, preventing crowding, urban decay, and keeping the city green and gardened. Seattle did not suffer the abandonment, blight, and disastrous urban renewal that hit eastern and midwestern cities at midcentury as their economies and demographics changed.

As the final frontier city of the lower forty-eight states, Seattle has always attracted adventurers and innovators, risk-takers, and those with an eye on the future. Seattle culture might be characterized overall by a socially and economically diverse population and thriving counterculture, all underwritten by gritty industrial origins.

ENDNOTES

1. Roger Sale, *Seattle: Past and Present: An Interpretation of the Foremost City of the Pacific Northwest* (Seattle: University of Washington Press, 1976), 4. Seattle's average annual rainfall is less than most eastern cities; however, the cloud cover and fog running from late fall to spring create a pervasive dampness that is difficult to endure.

2. Since 2004, Central Connecticut State University has compiled a list of "most literate" cities in the US, based the reading habits and resources of more than eighty US cities. The study considers the number of bookstores in a city, the population's educational attainment, newspaper circulation, library resources, and more. Seattle is consistently near the top of the list, placing second to Washington, DC, in 2017.

3. Charles Fischer, "Seattle's Disappearing Bookstores," *Seattle Magazine*, print edition, October 2013, web: http://www.seattlemag.com/article/seattles-disappearing-bookstores, accessed September 6, 2019.

4. John Koenig, *Dictionary of Obscure Sorrows*, https://www.dictionaryofobscuresorrows.com, accessed November 11, 2019.

5. Robert Gebelhoff, "We Are Living in a New Gilded Age: 2018 Proves It," the *Washington Post*, December 28, 2018, https://www.washingtonpost. com/opinions/2018/12/28/we-are-living-new-gilded-age-proves-it, accessed October 10, 2018.

6. See Shoshana Zuboff, *The Age of Surveillance Capitalism: The Fight for a Human Future at the New Frontier of Power* (New York: Hachette Book Group, 2019). Zuboff is professor emerita at Harvard Business School. *Surveillance capitalism* is defined by Zuboff, in part, as "a new

economic order that claims human experience as free raw material for hidden commercial practices of extraction, prediction, and sales."

7. Gene Balk, "The Decade in Demographics: The Top 5 Changes in the Seattle Area," Seattle Times, December 30, 2019, https://www.seattletimes.com/seattle-news/data/the-decade-in-demographics-seattles-top-5-changes/, accessed January 11, 2020.

8. Noah Buhayar and Dina Bass, "How Big Tech Swallowed Seattle," *Bloomberg News*, August 30, 2018, https://www.bloomberg.com/news/features/2018-08-30/how-big-tech-swallowed-seattle, accessed October 19, 2018.

9. The United Nations' most dire report yet on the climate crisis was released in October 2018. Seattle's (usually) miraculously clean and comfortable summer air was choked with smoke from regional forest fires in 2017 and 2018, although that was a small tragedy compared with those who suffered and died in the actual fires. Washington State governor Jay Inslee ran for the 2020 presidency on a platform entirely devoted to addressing the climate crisis, leaving the race on August 22, 2019.

10. Sara Ayad and Roderick Cave, *The History of the Book in 100 Books: The Complete Story, from Egypt to E-book* (Buffalo: Firefly Books, 2014), 12.

11. Ayad and Cave, *The History of the Book in 100 Books*, 12, 122.

12. Kelly Jensen, "Spokane Eliminates School Librarians, Continuing Trend of Disappearing School Libraries," *Book Riot*, April 16, 2019, https://bookriot.com/2019/04/16/eliminating-schoollibrarians, accessed September 25, 2019.

13. Jamie Lutton, quoted in Charles Fischer, "Seattle's Disappearing Bookstores," *Seattle Magazine*, October 2013.

14. Andria Cheng, "Bookstores Find Growth as Anchors of Authenticity," *New York Times*, June 23, 2019, https://www.nytimes.com/2019/06/23/business/independent-bookstores.html, accessed September 6, 2019.

15. See Jane Jacobs, *The Death and Life of Great American Cities* (New York: Vintage Books / Random House, 1961). For an overview of her activism and legacy, see Anthony Flint, *Wrestling with Moses: How Jane Jacobs Took On New York's Master Builder and Transformed the American City* (New York: Random House Trade Paperbacks, 2009).

16. Michael S. Rosenwald, "In the Age of Amazon, Used Bookstores Are Making an Unlikely Comeback," *Washington Post*, December 26, 2015, https://www.washingtonpost.com/local/in-the-age-of-amazon-used-bookstores-are-making-an-unlikely-comeback/2015/12/26/, accessed September 27, 2019.
17. Doug Schwartz, "Another Life for Twice Sold Tales," *Capitol Hill Seattle Blog*, October 1, 2009, https://www.capitolhillseattle.com/2009/10/another-life-for-twice-sold-tales/, accessed September 6, 2019.
18. Charles Fischer, "Seattle's Disappearing Bookstores," October 2013.
19. Posted by @madamemazzig, reposted March 18, 2019 on Magus Books Facebook page.
20. "Richard Leffel Obituary," *The Seattle Times*, February 13, 2011, web: https://www.legacy.com/obituaries/seattletimes/obituary.aspx?n=richard-leffel&pid=148544459, accessed January 10, 2020.
21. Cheng, "Bookstores Find Growth as Anchors of Authenticity," *New York Times*, June 23, 2019. The Association of American Publishers reports that sales of digital books fell 3.6 percent to $1.02 billion in 2018, a third straight decline, while hardback sales rose 6.9 percent to $3.06 billion and paperback sales 1.1 percent to $2.67 billion.
22. Semiotics, unlike semantics, includes the study of non-linguistic sign systems.
23. Liz Button, "Owner of Seattle's Arundel Bookstore Seeks Neighbor," *American Booksellers Association*, https://www.bookweb.org/news/owner-seattle's-arundel-books-seeks-bookstore-neighbor-35954, April 12, 2017, accessed September 6, 2019.
24. Michael Lieberman, "Al-Mutanabi street, Baghdad's Book Row, Gets its First Female Bookseller," *Book Patrol: A Haven for Book Culture*, March 24, 2015, http://bookpatrol.net/al-mutanabi-street-baghdads-book-row-gets-its-first-female-bookseller/, accessed January 10, 2019.
25. Levi Pulkkinnen, "Seattle's Bohemian Culture Struggles to Survive as Tech Takes Over: Amazon Fuels a Changing Landscape," *The Guardian*, July 20, 2018.
26. The Needling, "Fremont Troll Priced Out of Fremont, Moves to Tukwila," http://theneedling.com/2018/10/21/fremont-troll-priced-out-of-fremont-moves-to-tukwila/, accessed January 10, 2020.
27. Eli Pariser, "Beware of Online Filter Bubbles," TED2011 Talk, March 2011.

28. Roger McNamee, *Zucked: Waking Up to the Facebook Catastrophe* (New York: Penguin Press, 2019), 10. McNamee, a thirty-five-year veteran of Silicon Valley investing, was an early investor in Facebook and advisor to its CEO, and at the time of writing, still holds shares of the company. He "woke up" during and after the 2016 presidential election cycle. He writes, "Beginning with television, technology has changed the way we engage with society, substituting passive consumption of knowledge and ideas for civic engagement, digital communication for conversation. (...) A transformation that crept along for 50 years accelerated dramatically with the introduction of internet platforms. We were prepared to enjoy the benefits, but unprepared for the dark side."
29. Nicholas Kardaras, *Glow Kids: How Screen Addiction Is Hijacking Our Kids, and How to Break the Trance* (New York: St. Martin's Press, 2016), 4.
30. John Oliver, "Journalism," *Last Week Tonight with John Oliver*, August 7, 2016.
31. Jeffrey Kluger, "How Storytelling Makes Us Human," *Time*, December 5, 2017, web:https://time.com/5043166/storytelling-evolution/, accessed January 10, 2020.
32. Kardaras, *Glow Kids*, 4.
33. Meghan Cox Gurdon, "The Secret Power of the Children's Picture Book," *Wall Street Journal*, https://www.wsj.com/articles/the-secret-power-of-the-childrens-picture-book-11547824940, accessed September 24, 2019.
34. Heidi Bohan, *The People of Cascadia: Pacific Northwest Native American History* (Chesterfield: Mira Digital Publishing, 2009), 13.
35. Chief Seattle, "Statement on Surrendering Tribal Lands to Washington Territory Governor Isaac Stevens," 1854. *The Suquamish Foundation*, https://suquamish.nsn.us/home/about-us/chief-seattle-speech/, accessed August 23, 2019. The quote continues, "but that time long since passed away with the greatness of tribes that are now but a mournful memory."
36. "Top Ten Construction Projects of the Century in Washington State. Denny Regrade: Hosing Seattle into Shape," *Daily Journal of Commerce*, December 9, 1999, https://www.djc.com/special/century/10060862.htm, accessed August 26, 2019.
37. David B. Williams, "Olmstead Parks in Seattle," *History Link*, Essay 1124, May 10, 1999, https://www.historylink.org/File/1124, accessed August 26, 2019.

www.ingramcontent.com/pod-product-compliance
Lightning Source LLC
LaVergne TN
LVHW041612070526
838199LV00052B/3118